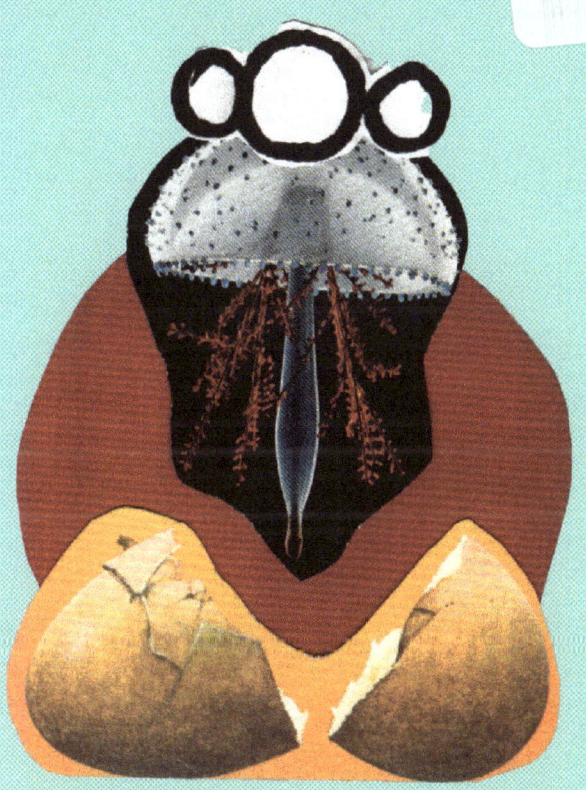

LITERARY KITCHEN / RURAL LIFE PRESS

Permission for the New Age Enthusiast

*How To Drop the Dogma of
Your Spiritual Practices & Set Yourself Free*

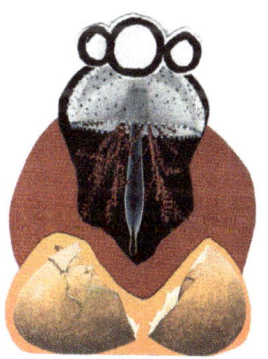

Written and Illustrated by
JEN ANTILL

Permission for the New Age Enthusiast:
How to Drop the Dogma of Your Spiritual Practices & Set Yourself Free
Copyright © 2024 by Jen Antill

All rights reserved. No portion of this publication may be reproduced in any form with the exception of reviewers quoting short passages, without the written permission of the publisher.

Published in 2024 by Rural Life Press, an imprint of Literary Kitchen
PO BOX 25
Chamisal, NM 87521
jenleighantill.com

ISBN: 978-1-950272-26-6

Cover art and interior illustrations: Jen Antill
Cover and interior design: Jenny Kimura
Design services provided by Indigo: Editing, Design, and More

Dedication

This book is dedicated to my own passionately hungry soul. You have never let me stop seeking or stop hunting growth. Sometimes you are a relentless beast but I love you anyway.

See below – me dressed up for Sunday school (I have been in some kind of spiritual community since I was five) circa 1990. Note: glasses do not contain lenses.

Appreciations

Thank you to Ariel Gore for supporting this chapbook and for helping me get it off the ground. Thank you for encouraging me to become and live as a radical writer who is true to her own voice. I have so much gratitude for all the books, zines and words you have put out into the world. You inspire me.

I want to send out a special thank you to my local Northern New Mexico community and their contributions of magazines that provided the images for this chapbook. Especially, the women at Art for the Heart in Peñasco, Judy Nelson who gifted me with over 300 birthday cards from her 93rd birthday and to Elizabeth Mascareñas in Dixon. Y'all have a special place in this chapbook.

To everyone who read this chapbook before it was published—thank you for your feedback and your genuine support. To Beth Lee and Laura Hitt—you helped me feel brave enough to keep going. And to my wife, who has no choice but to listen to me read to her at night when we are sitting on the couch by the fire, thank you for being my first editor and for always encouraging me to be even more honest.

Most importantly, to everyone I have met along the way in spiritual circles and communities—your stories and experiences have helped me understand how this New Age world is impacting all of us. Thank you for trusting me with your stories and with your healing. Thank you for believing that together, we can find a way to deeper truth. The recovery process from the New Age world is real and I see you. I'm so with you.

Sections

How to Read This Book	xi
Who This Book Is For	xiii
Before You Begin	xvii
I Do *Not* Say Daily Affirmations	1
Dat Lion's Gate Portal Though	7
Healer Splurge	11
Don't Mistake Your Man for the Divine Masculine	17
I'm Passing on Contact Improv	25
Spiritual DMing	31
Let the Queer World In	37
It's Already Done: The Illusion of Manifestation	45
The Obsession with Shadow	53
What If It Means Nothing / Shouldn't I Be Grateful?	61
Bonus Section: How the New Age World Reminds Me of Barbieland	67

How to Read This Book

My concept for this book is much like a tarot deck. (How New Age of me right?) I want you to be able to flip to any section and start there. *See where your flip takes you.* Of course, read as much into this as you want. If you don't like what you have flipped to, choose something else. Most importantly, there is no right way to read this book. We are letting go of dogma here.

My hope is for you to read this book and feel more permission for yourself—more freedom. My hope is that this book sits on your coffee table or on the dashboard of the van you're living in and when friends come to visit you, you give it to them to read. My hope is that you read it together and laugh aloud, recognizing yourself in these pages.

But ultimately, how you read this book is up to you, and that is a good place for us to begin.

Who This Book Is For

Anyone can read this book, of course.

I want anyone who wants to read these words to read them.

But ultimately I have written this book for cisgender women, meaning those of us who were assigned female at birth and then collectively socialized as women.

Still, in most spiritual communities, cisgender men are looked to as the dominant power and authority. If you identify as non-binary or are transmasculine, you may also identify with these stories as many of us raised with female conditioning in the Western world learn to doubt our own knowing in exchange for the promise of belonging and acceptance.

If you have never spent extensive time in the New Age world, then some of these experiences may be foreign or unknown to you. It is my hope, that even if you do not know this world well, you will still be able to find enough of an anchor in the overall permission of this book. After all, those of us who live in the Western world can usually use some encouragement to put down rigid systems that are ultimately founded on the structures of colonization and patriarchy.

This book is also focused on the experience of the New Age world in North America and may resonate most with my North American friends. These ideas may be alive and well wherever the New Age world has taken hold but I haven't yet been all over the world investigating this inquiry. That might be another adventure for another time.

And finally, if you find yourself feeling ashamed that you are not living a life that is the "most healthy" or "the most awake" then this book is for you. If you find yourself grabbing at any and all self-help material, if you are always pushing yourself to be on the verge of another spiritual breakthrough and if you are tired of trying so hard, then this book is for you. I know that place. I know that pressure. I hope to bring some levity to our situation. Let's do this.

Before You Begin

I am a New Age world enthusiast.
I grew up in an Evangelical Christian church in downtown Phoenix, Arizona. I was devoted and committed to Jesus from a young age — praying, getting baptized (I have been baptized three times because once did not seem like enough), trying to memorize Bible versus and working for years as a missionary on the inner city streets of Phoenix. After I left the church (that is another story), I went to Maui and learned about organic farming, non-violent communication and how to put crystals outside when the moon is full. My time in Maui was the first time I saw that spirituality existed outside of the confines of organized religion. I then moved to New Mexico where I joined a Shamanic community that I was

part of for seven years and then lived in Sedona, Arizona for two years which is (in my opinion) a Spiritual Disneyland for curious tourists.

I should also tell you that I am a psychotherapist and professional astrologer. I have also studied massage therapy, mystical midwifery, herbal medicine, Shamanic journeying and by all accounts, I am very much a witch. New Age communities have been my home and more than ever, I feel like I spend a lot of my time with myself, my friends and my clients unraveling harmful messages given to us by New Age communities and the professionals that work in them.

I have tried my hardest to heal myself of my pain, trauma and my broken history. I have tried to shut the darkness out and replace it with the light. I have tried to wake up, ascend and become whole only to find out that that quest is a trap. What my spiritual journey has led me to (so far) is the impossibility of shutting out my trauma and instead, replacing it with deep acceptance of who I am and where I come from. Instead of trying to ascend, I am left with trying to be human and to love myself for all of my imperfections.

This is my first adventure into writing about these topics. As I shared this writing with others, I came to realize that this material can and will be more than a chapbook. I have decades of experience inside of religious and spiritual communities to process, unravel and integrate. I know it will be one of the big explorations of my lifetime and one that I am honored to do through the written word. I am eagerly anticipating the process of deepening into the nuances of my story in future writing but for now, I offer you permission, humor and lightness. I offer you a bitesize chapbook — a beginning.

What is "New Age"?

For the purposes of this small book you hold in your hands, I want to tell you what I mean by *New Age*. To me, the New Age movement is defined by the ways that we seek to find spiritual meaning and purpose in our lives and the ways we seek connection to something larger than ourselves outside of wide spread forms of religious practices. Including, but not limited to: Judaism, Christianity, Mormonism, Catholicism, Hinduism, Buddhism and so on. The New Age movement is about creating something *different*, something most notoriously attractive to Self-Identified Seekers.

But many others have defined the New Age movement as well. The New Age movement (or NAM as some call it) has been described as a movement that is focused on spiritual transformation — a movement where people want to see society transform from one rooted in violence, war, racism and poverty into a society where peace, abundance and brotherly love are dominant. (We are optimists, to say the least.)

In the United States, the New Age movement gained momentum in the 1960s and 1970s when counterculture rose in popularity. Along with fighting for civil rights, many people in America were protesting the Vietnam War, doing a ton of psychedelics and of course, learning about transcendental meditation from our British friends: *The Beatles*. The New Age movement became interested in Indigenous practices belonging to Native American communities such as sweat lodges, pipe ceremonies and hanging dreamcatchers above beds all over America—seeking something outside of traditional, secular religious practices. The New Age movement also began to dip its toe into ancient Pagan/Celtic rituals such as Samhain and Beltane—circling back to earth-based traditions.

Most people drawn to the New Age movement seem to be largely interested in healing trauma and being pattern breakers of harmful family cycles. Many of us who show up to these communities are in pain and this makes us a particularly vulnerable lot. We want to believe there is a cure for our suffering and our discontent and because of that, we may be prone to believe a lot of things that in a more regulated state (meaning, when we're not triggered, anxious, agitated or afraid that we might never feel better), we would never entertain.

Many of us coming to the New Age movement are also outsiders and outcasts. We have left churches, other spiritual groups, families, communities and so on. We have gone in search of a different way of life. We know the feeling of isolation, lack of connection and feeling untethered and without a place to belong. In many ways, New Age circles promise us a sense of belonging to something that hopefully feels less dogmatic, more accepting and therefore, more free.

But with that freedom comes a risk. With that freedom comes our own blind spots, our own limitations and our own dogmatic ways of thinking that were born out of the colonized and patriarchal culture we were raised in. We try and make up new rules, better rules, but rules just the same. We try and name what is healthy. We try and name what spiritual mastery is and then, we are no more free than when we began. It is just another rule book with a rose quartz on the cover. It is my hope that we can start to name where the lines between the New Age movement and fundamentalism have become blurred and walk ourselves back to real freedom.

Everything in Dosage

Taken in the correct dosage and within the right context, many of the practices and activities throughout this chapbook are not inherently bad or something I would dissuade anyone from doing. There is something, however, that happens in New Age communities that seems to take innocent pieces of advice (like writing daily affirmations) and turn them into full blown dogmatic rituals. I have witnessed over the years, an adherence to advice in the New Age world that borders on the line of *obsession*.

There seems to be something in those of us interested in New Age communities that fears falling short, doing it wrong and staying stagnant and stuck. Because of this, I often find more black and white thinking in New Age circles. When we take these simple suggestions for feeling better (daily affirmations, making vision boards or pulling tarot cards) and blow them way out of proportion, we start to see, what I believe, is a very strangled version of what these activities were initially intended for.

If you have a healthy relationship with daily affirmations or pulling tarot cards, good for you. You do not need to be in recovery from the New Age world. But many of us are (or have been) avid addicts of the New Age world, seeking to be praised and affirmed for our rightness and our spiritual authority. ***This is when we need help.*** This is when we need support and permission to drop our spiritual competitiveness and learn to be human once more.

I Do *Not* Say Daily Affirmations

I have never been one to look in the mirror in the morning and say affirmations to myself. I have never written affirmations down in my journal and I do not have them placed on sticky notes around my room. It's not that I am against affirmations (I keep love notes from my wife on my bulletin board and these serve as affirmations for me) but I do think affirmations are highly over emphasized in the New Age world.

I do not want us to think that affirmations alone are the pathway to building self-love and self-esteem. Affirmations are a tool. They can be helpful sometimes, in some moments. But honestly, affirmations do not do much for me. Are affirmations going to heal and cure decades of crippling self-doubt and self-criticism? Probably not. Are affirmations going to help when we have experienced parents who subtly manipulated or shamed us for decades? Nah. I doubt it.

One time, back when I was deep in my spiritual cult days, I was at a weekend workshop on Shamanic journeying and I was very, very triggered. There was this girl, you see, and she was flirting with my girlfriend. And actually, my girlfriend was flirting back. This was not something that only happened once—it had been continuously happening for months and months. I am talking about aggressive, public flirting. I am not one of those people who says to my partner, *"Flirting is a natural part of who we are and I want you to feel like you can express yourself."* I am much more like, *"I must be the ONLY woman who you find attractive and endearing for all of eternity and I don't care if that's not considered healthy, it's what I need."* I get jealous. I get possessive and yes, I have read about the concept of compersion.

Instead of walking out of the workshop (which I absolutely needed to have done) I tried to "be the bigger person." More accurately, I tried to deny my feelings and force myself to feel calm when all I wanted to do was stab both my girlfriend and the girl she was flirting with in the neck. I tried to quiet my rage and calm myself, but nothing worked.

The more I sat inside my circle altar (that I built with stones and sprinkled with tobacco and cornmeal in order to honor the Spirits), the more shut down and angry I felt.

In-between Shamanic journeys (which were done inside our circle altars) I went and stood outside among the piñon and juniper trees. I took deep breaths, I reminded myself that people loved me and I let the New Mexico sun shine upon my face, something that usually always cheers me up. But still, I felt jealous, enraged and completely walled-off.

Finally, the 60-year-old facilitator (who was someone I was inappropriately close with at the time and who was also my therapist—let's talk about zero boundaries!) handed me a folded-up sticky note with an affirmation written on it. It read,

You are irreplaceable.

This did nothing to calm me down. I held the sticky note in my hand all day and read it over and over again, hoping it would assuage the rage and jealousy I felt inside of me. After all *someone* loved me, someone felt I was irreplaceable. But there was nothing the sticky note could do. It was not enough. I just didn't believe it.

Affirmations do not change deeply rooted emotional and psychological patterning. They don't need to. If you feel like your daily affirmations are not working, it is most likely because they are *not* working. They should never have been enough to change your core emotional wounding. You're not doing it wrong, it's just that the sticky notes are not enough. I'm sorry if your therapist or your life coach or an Instagram Influencer told you they would be. I'm sorry if that sticky note on your bathroom mirror that tells you to remember your body is perfect the way it is is not working out for you. That sticky note is up against collective conditioning and a dominant narrative that has been around for centuries.

One sticky note does not a paradigm change.

Let your sticky notes be colorful. By all means, get those bright blue and purple ones. I love those. But if you come into therapy and apologize for not feeling better because you have not been doing your daily affirmations, then our culture of spiritual and psychological consumerism has done you a disservice. Lack of daily affirmations is not why you're feeling bad. I am not going to get into all the reasons you are

PERMISSION FOR THE NEW AGE ENTHUSIAST

probably feeling sad or heavy or depressed on some days but again, it is not from a lack of sticky-noting. The pressure in our New Age world to have proudly decorated sticky notes in our intimate spaces is a lot.

If I were to have one sticky note up, it would probably say:

*It's okay that you don't have any
sticky note affirmations up.
You do you girl.*

Dat Lion's Gate Portal Though

Please stop waiting for the Lion's Gate Portal on 8/8 to let go of the past and ask yourself what kind of forward movement you'd like to make. (Either you're Googling it now or you know exactly what I'm talking about.) Honestly, I just found out what this whole Lion's Gate Portal thing was about and I'm an astrologer so a lot of people were very shocked that I did not know what it was. For those of you who are unfamiliar, the Lion's Gate Portal coincides with the season of Leo in astrology. Because of its relationship to Leo season, the Lion's Gate Portal advises us to spend some time with our inner child and ask how that inner child would like to create our future. In theory, this doesn't sound like a bad practice but y'all there is A LOT of emphasis on this day in New Age communities.

Dedicating one day of our lives to chatting with our inner child and deciding what we want for our future is like walking down the altar, blindfolded to someone we've never met. What if you don't feel like doing *anything* on 8/8? What if we're sick that day or feel super depressed? What if we don't take advantage of this miraculous portal? What if trying to come up with what we want is one of the hardest things anyone can ever ask us to do because we're still trying to learn how to give ourselves permission to *want*?

You can hone your future on 11/6 or 3/24. You can do it any day and every day. You don't have to wait until the clock says 11:11 (I SEE you). You can do it whenever you want and you can *not* do it whenever you want. *You're* a portal. How about that? You're an ever-evolving portal that has access to your future when you're ready and when the timing is right for you. Better yet, let finding out about that future of yours be an on-going practice, one that goes on for the rest of your life.

You also do not have to know what the Lion's Gate Portal is. This does not make you a bad witch. Unless you grew up in ancient Egypt (maybe one of your past life regressions told you that you did), you probably don't have much experience observing this particular portal. The Lion's Gate Portal was most likely not part of your family culture growing up in the late 20th century. It definitely was not part of mine. My family culture was more like tape decks and El Camino's. My family culture was Paul Simon and NPR (yes, obviously I am white).

    I believe in portals. I believe in astrological transits. I believe in eclipse season and energy that is stronger now and less intense tomorrow. I believe in it all. But let's go easy on this Lion's Gate Portal. If all of your karmic debts are not released on that day and if your inner child is not forever healed, there are going to be many more opportunities.

Healer Splurge

If you are seeing more than two different kinds of healers at the moment, I want you to stop. I know that therapy, breath work, astrology, human design, sound healing, Ayurveda, kinesiology, mediumship, past life regression, cord cutting, Shamanism, medicine journey circles, mindful meditation and cacao heart opening ceremonies are all super intriguing. But let's just say that if you're doing more than two of these things, you're doing too much.

Do you send away in the mail for someone to tell you about your birthday numerology or analyze your handwriting? Are you waiting for your magical body worker (who, by the way, feels like they have known you in other lifetimes) to tell you why your throat chakra is closed?

JEN ANTILL

You may be obsessed with healing.

You may be certain that if you try enough healers, there may be some cure that will rid you of the pain you carry around with you. I am gonna tell you something that you probably won't like:

There is no cure.

I sent away for my first astrology reading when I was 13 and still have it in my file cabinet. (Yes, the reading was handwritten and I have it stored in a turquoise file cabinet in my room.) I started seeing a therapist when I was seven. I have been into this healing business for a long time.

But, there are no short cuts and there are no roundabout ways. There is no quick and dirty, one-time session to heal all Wrongs of the Soul. We may gather insights, awareness and temporary relief but the Great Mystery will always come back for collections. It will always call us back to the places that are painful and uncertain — this is the only thing that seems to be certain. That, and death of course.

There are so many different kinds of healers. Some of them do REALLY interesting things in session. Some of what they say feels really accurate. And a lot of what they say can and does send us into an anxious spiral — down dark rabbit holes of psychological confusion. We may start to feel the cacophony of voices from healers past in our heads and we may begin to feel conflicted as to which one to listen to. We may lose the pulse on our own voice and our own knowing. *What my acupuncturist said conflicts with what my Reiki practitioner said. My therapist said something different than my tarot reader and my life coach pointed me in a whole other direction.*

This is psychological exhaustion.

At best, I think we can hope for one or two Wise Voices in our lives — ones that we build trust and rapport with *over time*. (It takes time for us to understand how people think, what their values are and how they respond to us when we're in pain.) Those Wise Voices are the ones that become the figures in our dreams who appear on the side of a dark mountain road holding a lantern — the ones even our Unconscious knows to trust.

"BUT…" you say —

"I *like* when a total stranger peers into my Akashic Record and tells me (accurately) the story of my life. I *like* when the Vedic Astrologer tells me which planets are exalted in my chart!"

If you must, get your fix—dive into your Healer Splurge.

When you're itching for that illusive clarity and you book a random session with a psychic (never have I ever done this) and then she tells you that you have blocks to intimacy (who me?!) and you definitely and most certainly feel worse about yourself than before the session, you know it's time to stop.

You don't need one more session, one more healing or one more exorcism. You are good, for now. I promise there will be more healing to come. There is more in your future. There is more to know but for now, maybe just take a nap.

Don't Mistake Your Man for the Divine Masculine

A Quick Note:

This section is particularly for women who identify as heterosexual: cisgender women who love cisgender men. Please do read on if you do not identify in this way but this particular challenge seems to lie with my straight lady friends. I am bisexual (you can flip to the section called: "Let the Queer World In" and read more about this) and do understand the challenges in this section. I have spent many a year dating men, loving men and thinking about how to manifest the best kind of masculine spiritual hero so here we go.

There is this illusive beast called: *The Divine Masculine*. You have not met him yet but when you do, he is going to be financially stable, physically fit, emotionally intelligent and also a practitioner of some sort of Taoist tradition. And he'll definitely help you raise the child you had with another man because he has not committed to anything yet and has no ex-wives or other children. He has been living in Peru, doing ayahuasca in the jungle and living in a small hut, swimming in the ocean every day until he met *you*. And now he is ready to sip peyote with you in a slightly bigger jungle hut and build you that outdoor kitchen you have always wanted. And he is good with his hands, obviously. I mean, he just turned an old, rotting shed into a recording studio where he can now record hang drum music and post it on his YouTube channel.

This Divine Masculine is the King to your Queen and don't worry Sister, he's out there for you. You only have to cut the cords with your ex-husband and then he will be a match to your energy.

FINALLY.

He will appear, with his shirt off, exposing his stonewashed abdomen and smelling slightly of B vitamins. He will know how to use

I-Statements and he will never, ever gaslight you. He will tilt his head to the side when listening to you and slightly smile. He will tell you how beautiful you are and always let you choose what movie to watch. (He probably hasn't even seen a movie in over a decade because he has been too busy meditating.)

IN REALITY...
The Divine Masculine is an archetype.
This means, it is a pattern—a non-human form, an idea,
an image, a quality that exists in myths and stories.

A lot of us queer folk have already accepted that our myth of romance and the spell of heterosexual normatively will eventually be broken. We do not have what was promised to us by this Western culture and we have started to create a rainbow-colored paradigm of love. But I fear that my New Age heterosexual amigas are still holding onto a world where their man should appear to be more than human.

The thing about real, human men is this: they are going to smell weird when they eat bad food, they are going to become avoidant (some of the time), they are going to get it wrong, fuck it up, hurt you, disappoint you, frustrate you and hide parts of themselves from you. They are going to text their ex-girlfriend and not tell you, they are going to scream at your kid one day and they are going to forget to get the organic, overnight pads with wings that you explicitly asked them for. It is going to be very unromantic. It is going to be so day-to-day. It is going to be mundane and boring as hell.

I want you to know that if your man does not come to you in the form of a centaur wearing medallions and a crown of flowers, you're not getting it wrong. If you meet your dude on Hinge or at a bowling alley, that's great. No man in a partnership can withstand the pressure of fulfilling the role of the Divine Masculine. When women tell other women that they have found the Divine Masculine, it makes most of us feel badly. It makes most people feel like there is some relationship goal out there that they are supremely failing at.

But the good news is, this means you do not have to be a Queen—you also get to be human. You do not *always* have to stand in your power and be a badass warrior mama. You get to put the scepter down and take off the jeweled robe (unless you're playing dress up then go for it). You don't have to always be in alignment or speak your truth. You get to fuck up too.

Let the Gods live in their myths. Let the Gods roam the pages of stories and legends. Let your guy be human. He is not the Divine Masculine — he is a man. And men were once little boys who ran around melting beetles with magnifying glasses on the sidewalk. He is not going to float down to you on a cloud of quinoa and zucchini squash and know how to love you. You are going to have to teach him so much. And he is going to have to teach you so much.

Our Western culture failed at teaching us about love and so we turned to the ancient mystics (I know you want to quote Rumi to me right now) to teach us about romance and love and they got it wrong too. They didn't tell us how real love was going to be and that there would be so many weird smells that go along with it. They didn't tell us that sex can be awkward, with so many elbows and knees. They told us to expect Ghandi and Buddha and Sexy Bearded Jesus in the 21st century — men who were committed to moral principles that no mortal can uphold.

I'm all for high standards and weeding out the losers that come and go from our dating lives. I'm all for telling that dude who promises (AT ANY MOMENT) that he is going to apply for that barista job but hasn't gotten around to it yet, that he needs to forget he has your number. I'm all for walking away and blocking people who do not support us and ultimately, make our lives better.

But please don't ask your man to be a King.

Ultimately, Kings get dethroned, murdered, start wars and sleep with their mothers. Or so the legends go. Ask him to be human and gentle and kind. Ask him to listen and to apologize. Ask him to care about the things that are important to you. Take him off the throne. This will make all the flaws so much less shocking when they emerge.

And don't tell me you are going to start sleeping with women because there are no good men out there for you.

I met a dude last night at dinner who was single and even had a man bun. His name was Davyd and I think you'll like that he replaced the "i" with a "y." He seems available and like your type. What about Davyd?!

If you want to start sleeping with women, by all means, please do. I think it's pretty fantastic. You don't need the excuse that you've run out of Kings to your Queen. You can just do it because you want to and because that girl from the juicery is definitely flirting with you and it's time you got her number.

I'm Passing on Contact Improv

I **don't want to go to contact improv tonight or on the** following Wednesday either. I don't want to look deeply into a stranger's eyes (a stranger that is most likely a 65-year-old man with a medium-long ponytail hanging down his back) and try to match my movements with theirs, or feel their sweaty hand on the small of my back. I don't want to try and "dance like no one is watching" while I can feel the older gentleman eyeing me from across the room. HE IS WATCHING OKAY? I don't want to make a longterm eye contact commitment with anyone. I don't want to slide my thigh across someone's abdomen and see if it helps me process childhood trauma.

I know I might seem like I enjoy contact improv and maybe even ecstatic dance because I am into some of the New Age things that you are into. I know we've seen each other at the local vegan chocolate shop (I'm not a vegan, they just have delicious chocolate) and you've seen me looking at astrology charts on my laptop but still, I'm passing on contact improv. I actually prefer to dance while listening to hip-hop and reggaetón, walking by myself down an old dirt road or on the mountain behind my house where there is absolutely *no one else* around.

 I do not want to go to contact improv to meet the community there or to ask a new friend what she feeds her kombucha starter. I want to dance alone, with my headphones in, listening to Beyoncé's *Lemonade* album on repeat. I want to think about the boys/girls who have done me wrong and work on my twerking.

 I do not want to be told that contact improv is a time to explore "free movement" and see where our body takes us. Listen, I have had severe constipation my entire life from having to exist in groups of people that made me uncomfortable. The last thing that feels relaxing and freeing to me is dancing in a room full of strangers who want to explore touching me in some kind of intimate way. I am one of those people who is INCREDIBLY sensitive to group energy. I can feel the vibe in the room and then I can and will feel every person and their combined trauma that they have carried for generations. So no, I am not going to be able to focus on rolling around on the ground to release my pelvic floor while next to me, I can feel the guy's grief from his recent break-up and how he is hoping to meet an emotionally intelligent woman at contact improv tonight that may or may not be me.

Contact improv always seems like something I *should* try. I mean, I am a theatre kid at heart. (GO THESPIANS!) It is similar to me thinking I should be an aerialist or a comedic clown. I should go to circus school right? The circus is definitely in now. It is cool to juggle and wear a clown nose and walk around on stilts, make puppets and teach small children how to talk about their emotions. When I was nine I asked for a unicycle for Christmas, got it and then learned how to ride it. Circus here I come.

I just don't think I want my healing to also have to be performative. I like to heal in the intimacy of my therapist's ZOOM room or by myself looking out the window of an airplane. I like my somatic releases to come while I am alone, or at least with someone who I have built a solid rapport with. And by solid rapport, I mean at least eight years of deep friendship. (I take a long time to warm up.) So no, I will not be going to contact improv tonight and I also will not be trying out that Intro to Aerial Silks Class you keep talking about. I am not agile or graceful and I most definitely do not have the upper body strength to pull myself up into a full body plank while floating 12 feet in the air.

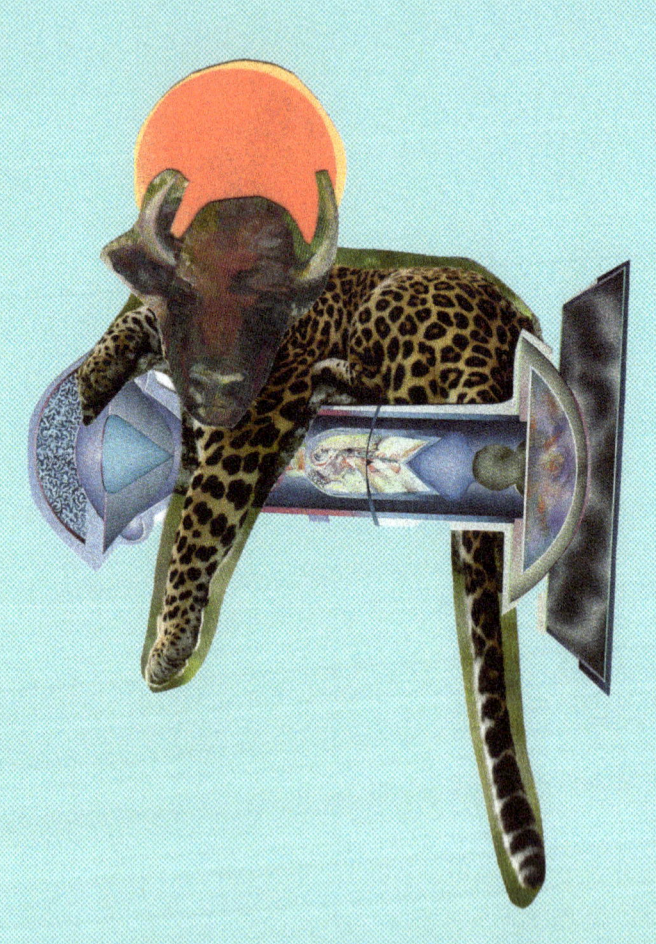

Spiritual DMing

Note:

This section will also mainly appeal to my cisgender lady friends and for the most part, those who "appear" heterosexual on social media — whatever *that* means.

Alright ladies, if a man approaches you in your DMs (sorry, I do not TIK TOK) and writes something like, *I am feeling called by Spirit to invite you into my group coaching program. I don't know why, it just feels right*. Please immediately block him and delete all messages from him. This is NOT a sign from

Source that you should work with him. You are not the one, special woman he is sending this message to on this particular evening. There are many other women and their names are Akasha, Luna, Abundyance and Matrixx. (Just to be clear, their real names are Jessica, Tiffany, Ashley and Emily.)

Please know that this is spiritual manipulation disguised as Instagram flattery and then covered up with some good ol' heavy-handed coercion. The reason this kind of messaging works is because WE ARE STILL hungry to hear that we are wanted, chosen, desired, special, unique and especially, destined to be part of something ordained by God, Spirit, Source, The Divine, Pacha Mama and so on. I will never fault you for this. It feels fucking good to be chosen—to be wanted. I don't care how "spiritually evolved" you are. If you are a woman in this world, you are still going to feel powerful when a man gives you attention. This is how almost all of us were socialized.

This man is trying to appeal to that exact tender spot in you that is vulnerable to his attention. He also wants CASH MONEY. He also wants a picture of your beautiful face on the testimonial wall on his website. He also wants his own version of validation that a beautiful woman like yourself wants to trust and work with him. IT'S ALL FOR HIM.

I can guarantee you that this man also wants to invite you to an ayahuasca retreat in Costa Rica that costs upward of $10,000, not including airfare and lodging. But to be certain, it will be with a REAL Shaman—one that he will give a very small percentage of his actual retreat income to because this REAL Shaman is from a rural village in Guatemala and did not take the time to ask how much this dude (Given Name: Mike. New Age name: Matador) was making off of his retreat.

I'll just say this to be clear as well: please do not do mushrooms with him or psychedelics of any kind—even if he says it will help you process your trauma. Block him and move away from your phone. Get him out of your life. You do not need him and your bank account certainly does not need him. You just saved yourself 10K and years of therapy to process the way he broke your trust after you were sure he was committed to helping you.

I'm sorry if this has happened to you. I'm sorry if this is currently happening to you. I'm sorry if you felt like you were investing in someone who was actually going to help you move forward with your very real and earnest business and instead, you ended up learning how to have boundaries and recognize red flag behavior. I know we are all STILL learning this ladies. You are not alone. I have been there so many times.

Receiving these kinds of slithery and slimy DMs reminds me of those messages from the bank that read something like:

If you are contacted by us any way other than via phone, it is a SCAM. It is NOT your real bank. Do not respond.

Unless YOU are reaching out to a spiritually-focused coaching program that looks promising to you or better yet, that comes highly recommended to you by a very trusted friend, delete the message. Entrepreneurs (claiming to have a "spiritual business") who slide into DMs and hungrily grasp at eager, barely off the ground, businesses run by kick-ass women do not deserve a response.

It will get easier and easier to recognize this kind of behavior. You will start to recognize that the adrenaline you feel in receiving a message like this is anxiety, warning you of the danger to come. You will start to trust your body that something just feels *off*. You will stop second guessing yourself and start becoming deeply skilled at recognizing this kind of sleazy behavior. And when he promises you healing along with his coaching package, know that he is right. There WILL be healing. It will just be *you* healing from the psychological damage he's done. It will be the healing you engage in while learning to reestablish your boundaries and reclaim your power.

Let the Queer World In

The language of the New Age world is largely geared toward cisgender, heterosexual, white women. Goddess Circles, Sister Circles, Sisterhood Retreats, Feminine Power and Shakti Energy are commonly used phrases in this world. This language, that is meant to feel empowering to so many women, *excludes the queer world* not to mention the non-white world. (Since I am white, I am not the racial voice of authority in this realm and will defer to other people's experiences who are, of course, not white.)

When we first moved to Sedona, Arizona, my wife got invited to Sisterhood Circles all the time. I was always shocked when people would ask me, "Isn't your wife going to come to Sisterhood Circle?" I had not even thought to ask my wife to come to Sisterhood Circle. Not because I want to exclude her from community but because the activities and essence of these Sisterhood Circles is so typically and culturally female that my wife would hate it. You want my wife to engage in slow, sensual hip circles while staring at herself in a mirror? You want my wife to place a jade yoni egg inside herself (while also watching fifteen other women strategically place theirs inside their yoni cavity) and meditate for twenty minutes?

NAAAAHHHHHHHH. HARD PASS TEAM.

What I also do not think cisgender, heterosexual women understand, is that if I bring my very butch and attractive wife to your Sisterhood Circle, you're going to develop a crush on her. She has a wide and generous smile, powerful green (sometimes blue) eyes, a full head of strong, Italian, wavy brown hair and a wicked tan. Every month, I cut her hair into a mohawk (I watched a YouTube video on cutting mohawks and now I'm an expert) and shave the sides of her head. My wife also used to be a division one basketball player and trained professional athletes. She is in shape. It will *not* be like bringing my femme, childhood gal pal, Kelly to Sisterhood Circle. You will start to feel things in your body and psyche that feel confusing to you (I promise). You will start to yearn.

I am bisexual. I can and do pass for straight ALL THE TIME. I have long, blonde hair and when I straighten it into submission and put on some eyeliner, my sexual orientation can be very confusing. When I tell people (mostly men) that I am married to a woman, I still get the, "Really?" response along with a head tilt. I can go to a Sisterhood Circle and then come home and chop wood and lay tile in my Carhartt overalls. I can live in both worlds which means, I get *exclusive* access to both worlds. It also means I don't quite fit in either world.

I am the queerest girl at the Sisterhood Circle and the straightest girl among my queer friends. I have accepted this fact about myself — this paradox about my sexuality.

If the New Age movement is the somewhat rebellious granddaughter of organized religion, then perhaps we need to look at the ancestral line. Many religions demonize relationships that are not heterosexual and ostracize people who are gender non-conforming. If the New Age movement is going to break some lineage patterns of religious fundamentalism, then we need to work on our inclusivity of the queer community.

Many queer people have already lost their communities and families. Many queer people have been rejected and cast aside from their places of belonging. As we drag our weary asses to the New Age table, we do not need yet another reason to feel that we have not been considered.

Most of the myths I read as part of my graduate program (yes, my graduate program included myth reading) revolved around heteronormative storylines and characters. There are queer-centered tarot decks *beginning* to emerge (thank you Cristy C. Road) but they are few and far between and don't get me started on the goddesses we queer folk are supposed to identify with. Perhaps Artemis is our closest queer ally in that she is a woman who is also a badass warrior, hunts with a bow and arrow and refuses to marry (a man).

Film and TV have made massive headway in regards to queer representation—it is time for the New Age world to follow suit. Innana makes her decent to live with Hades and Hera puts up with Zeus's misogyny for far too long. These stories leave us firmly planted in a heteronormative world with almost no windows that open into other realities.

It's time to find new stories.

Of course, I want my ladies to have those SUPER FREAKY FEMALE spaces where they can roll around on the floor and talk about all the sex with men they are having. I want there to be heterosexually focused spaces just like I want there to be spaces that focus on the lives and stories of queer folks. I want heterosexual, cisgender women to have spaces where there is absolutely no sexual energy present so that they can reveal themselves and unravel in ways that cannot happen when the gaze of their sexual desire is upon them. (Oh my GAWD, don't come for me here—I know that cisgender, femme women can be super attracted to one another and have amazing, erotic relationships together but also, when masculine energy *in any form* is present, women behave differently. I believe that this is due to the way that many women have been taught to compete with one another for the attention of the most masculine person in the room and to receive power through sexual and erotic currency.)

Many of my queer, butch and more androgynous friends who were socialized as straight, femme girls realized they did not identify with the characteristics that go along with those labels and ended up adopting some traditional "male characteristics." For example, not talking about their emotions, numbing their feelings and learning to be unaware of their bodies. This means that sitting in a circle with women and talking about their feelings, pulling tarot cards and speaking intentions out loud may feel completely and utterly inaccessible.

If you're a queer person who is trying to exist in the New Age world, I bet you have felt excluded but, at least not as excluded as you have in other circles. It might be a step toward more inclusivity and sometimes, because of that we might be willing to settle. At least we are not being told that we should burn in eternal damnation right?

We take what we can get.

I want to validate your discomfort, OUR discomfort, and say that the New Age world still has a long way to go. I know that it is up to me, up to us, to bring new stories, new tarot deck images, new rituals and new language to New Age circles. I am not expecting anyone else to do that. I know I am part of that bridge. I just don't want you to feel so alone if you've been feeling like you have to suck it up and at least be grateful there is a place you can exist that doesn't want you to die. It can be better, we can be better and I guess I just wanted to say, I'm starting.

It's Already Done: The Illusion of Manifestation

There is a magical saying in this New Age business — I'm sure you have heard it. When you say out loud that you want something, you need something or desire something, it is almost certain that someone sitting close to you with henna recently drawn on the backs of their hands will say, *"It is already done."* This is meant as a blessing. It is meant as a celebration of your ensured success. It is meant to adorn you with support and to set you up with Spirits on the Sidelines cheering you toward a goal you are sure to accomplish.

Back before my wife and I bought a small farm and homestead, we were living in Sedona, Arizona. Buying a small farm and homestead was the thing that I wanted MORE THAN ANYTHING ELSE in the world which meant, I talked about it a lot. One particularly warm and sunny Sedona day, I was sitting in a friend's backyard, in awe of the view from her porch. (If you've never been to Sedona, the red rocks there are truly magnificent. I mean, the place should be a national park, not a spot where people can roll out plastic lawn furniture and fake grass in their recently purchased townhouse.) We were, of course, having a potluck where vegan cream cheese made the rounds along with some kind of bird seed cracker. I had found a bright and dry spot on the "grass" where I could sit squarely in the sun, letting it warm my face and shoulders. As my friend approached me and sat down next to me (I don't think she had henna on her hands but she *was* wearing a purple Bindi), we got to talking about home and I quickly shared with her that I wanted to buy a small farm and homestead. She turned to me, looked directly into my eyes while smiling, grabbed my arm and said, "It is already done!" I recoiled inside but smiled back at her, assuring her that her affirmation was well taken.

In using this saying, we miss a very important step. In fact, we miss ALL the steps. We miss the in-between journey toward reaching our goal. We miss the struggle and the unexpected delights, we miss the challenges and the surprises along the way. We miss the event of actually getting to where we are going when it is "already done."

What if we didn't actually end up doing that thing? What if we get struck by lightning or put an axe through our hand when chopping wood? (My wife has NEVER done this.) What about accounting for the unknown and the unexpected? What happens when life changes our plans? I know we all wish Hogwarts was a real place and that with a sweep of our wand (EXPELIAMOS!) we could make appear in seconds what takes years and decades of perseverance.

In the world of magic, things are immediate and perfect.
In the world of humans, things are complicated, ambiguous
and take unknown quantities of time.

In the New Age world, the faster we can make something happen, the more in alignment we seem to be and the more Spirit seems to be helping us. If something takes time, effort and patience, we seem less likely to see the Hand of God at work. We are less likely to call it magic.

Instead of saying "It's already done" and snapping our fingers, can we lean in and ask one another what we might need in order to accomplish our goal? How can we help support one another in getting to where we want to go? What infrastructure needs to be built and laid down first so that we can begin and more importantly, continue our journey?

The New Age world seems to promote stories of overnight success when in fact, every time we hear an overnight success story amongst famous and well known people, when we look at where they were before they became "successful," we indeed see that it was a long road. Beyoncé's first job was working in her mother's hair salon where she would sweep the floors every day. Jimmy Fallon's first job was at a grocery store and Joni Mitchell's first job was working at a department store. My first job was cleaning out animal kennels at the vet—I would come home smelling like urine and blood, with animal feces stuck to the bottom of my red Converse low tops. We do not end up where we start and where we end up takes time, patience and endurance.

When people tell me that something is *already done*, I feel dismissed, rushed, hurried along. I feel a deep sadness settle into my bones that I cannot always explain. Don't you want to see how I get there? Don't you want to hear about my worries and fears and concerns along the way? Don't you want to sit me down and listen to how this dream I am trying to build will require the bravest parts of me and how I am terrified I won't be able to do it?

When we rush the process, we miss out on human relationship.

When we say that it's already done, we cut the conversation short. We stop one another mid-sentence. We break rhythm of what could be shared between two people. It is like telling a small, anxious child that *everything is going to be fine* and then walking out of the room. In reality, what that small child needs us to say is, "Sometimes I get scared too. I get it. It's okay that you're scared. Let's be scared together for a moment." They don't need to be rushed through their feelings. They need you (us) to be WITH them in their feelings—whatever they may be.

I don't need your reassurance. I don't need you to assuage my fears. I don't need your encouragement and I DEFINITELY don't need you to tell me not to be afraid. There is plenty to be afraid of and I want to feel all of it. No, I don't want to wallow in a hole of fear and second guessing myself, but I don't need you to tell me my fears are irrelevant. And just to be clear, you telling me it's "already done" does not make me less afraid. It does not magically bolster my confidence.

I want you to touch my tears and hear my stories. I want you to hug me and go hiking with me so I can talk about my journey. I want to be present to all the moments and chapters so that at the end we can look back and say we are proud of how we traversed this incredibly challenging and unpredictable road together, every step of the way.

So no, it's not *already done*. I am only beginning. And the way I feel your love and support for me is when you ask me how I'm going to make it through the journey.

The Obsession with Shadow

There is a reclamation around Sisterhood that seems to be happening in New Age communities. Everywhere I look (I look in very specific places), women (and again, I mostly mean cisgender and heterosexual women as well as, white women) are gathering in circles, they are potlucking, they are bringing back massage trains and they are chanting *Rising Appalachia* songs together by the fire. There seems to be a collective, female drive to create strong bonds with one another and to cultivate deep and sustained relationships. By the way, I think I tried to start the original Sisterhood Circle when I was in pre-school and convinced most of my friends (who were girls) that it would be cool if we were tongue sisters. What this meant is that I would convince my friends to meet me behind the playground so that we could touch tongues and be connected through our saliva for the rest of our lives. (I'm glad this was something that was still possible back in the 80s and not outlawed by overly cautious public health mandates.)

I think where many of us are getting confused in the world of Sisterhood, is that we seem to also want to use these circles as a way to call one another out on our shadow. These circles are being used as a way to "hold the mirror up" to one another and to try and fit others into our perception of what healing should look like. The only thing about holding mirrors up, is that *many* things have to be in place to make sure the person looking back at their reflection does not chuck the mirror out of the window or better yet, throw it at your head.

For example, when a woman shares something vulnerable in a circle (how she is still having trouble putting up boundaries with that asshole she dated three years ago), it usually (98% of the time) DOES NOT go well if someone then responds to her share with, "Can I offer you some advice?" Sure, you asked for consent but I bet ya she doesn't really want to hear what you have to say. I bet you she will vulnerably nod and say yes when in fact she means, DON'T YOU DARE SHAME ME IN FRONT OF THIS GROUP THAT I HAVE ONLY COME TO TWICE BEFORE.

She cannot guarantee that your advice will be loving or kind or considerate of her and her particular struggles. Why? Because you don't know her. You are about to throw out some conventional, band-aid advice that may or may not apply to her. You could get lucky. She could resonate with what you say but more often than not, you are going to project your life and your situation onto her instead of actually seeing *her* and her unique situation.

Please do not tell your fellow sister what she now needs to do to put up boundaries with her ex-boyfriend. She already knows she needs boundaries, that is why she is sharing about her lack of them. Please do not tell her that she is worthy and worth it and needs to believe she is lovable. She will most likely say, "Thank you," and smile but she will not really believe you, she won't be able to really take it in. Please do not tell her about all the work you've done around boundaries and please do not tell her how to have boundaries, why boundaries are important or what it looks like when you don't have them. This is not a teaching moment. This is not a moment to make yourself look good. This is the moment to simply listen to her and say, "Damn, that sounds hard. I'm here for you."

In order for someone to receive a message where they could even BEGIN to think about changing something unsettling about themselves, growing, implementing or integrating an uncomfortable place in their psyche, there would need to be a great deal of trust and safety present. In many Sisterhood Circles, suggestions are thrown into the communal stew without the proper ingredients. There is no trust or safety built. There is only the assumption that everyone wants to *quickly* grow and that means Call Out Culture is alive and well. We are calling out one another's shadow and we are doing it ruthlessly. We often cling to the comfort that this is for the good of our sister and if we do not tell her, who will?

Maybe no one will tell her. Maybe her therapist will tell her, maybe her good friend will tell her, maybe her partner will talk with her about it, maybe God will make it known to her or maybe no one will. Maybe this sister will not grow in the way you think she needs to. Maybe your agenda for the healing she needs to engage in will not be met. And maybe, most especially, maybe there is nothing wrong with our Dear Sister at all.

Let me tell you this Sisters:

If your body feels uncomfortable and you do not feel safe in a Sisterhood Circle, it is not you. It is the environment.

Most likely, that circle of well-meaning sisters has no idea how to create a space where safety can truly begin to grow.

Let's stop using our women-filled spaces as a place to call one another out and force each other to grow. I know it's tempting but it only recreates the message that we are lacking, not good enough and need to be better. AND DON'T WE GET THAT ENOUGH AS HUMANS—LET ALONE WOMEN?! This is how we perpetuate the agenda of spiritual fundamentalism. What if it wasn't your responsibility to make sure anyone rose to their highest spiritual potential? To see their shadow? To come to know their limitations? What if we could set that all down and just eat some food together, sit by a river and lay our heads in one another's laps, braiding each other's hair like old times?

Because New Age folks are usually a community of seekers, we want to grow and change and understand how we hold ourselves back. This is wonderful. I am like this too. But I only let a handful (mainly, my wife, dog and my therapist) call me out on things and have the permission in my life to be able to tell me when I'm being an asshole. Other people do not know me well enough nor have we built the safety required for them to speak into my life like this.

Perhaps there is a moment in time and culture when naming the shadow will feel appropriate once more. But for now, the shadow seems to get too much light. The hunt for the shadow so that we can eradicate it seems counterintuitive to me. It creates communities of hostility and resentment. It creates places where we do not feel safe to bring our most vulnerable material.

Technically, our shadow is the part of us that we cannot see. It lives underground, in the unconscious, in our dreams and in the recesses of our psyche. In my experience, there is no rushing what we are not aware of. There is only acceptance of what is until the shadow feels safe enough to come out.

If we rush the shadow, if we name it before it is ready, if we yell at it and tell it how it can fix itself, the shadow grows full of shame and becomes even more deeply committed to its original job.

Being able to see something in someone that they are unaware of is a gift.

This kind of awareness is a medicinal quality. If we do not use this gift with discretion, we ultimately create more damage than we do good.

Most of us, who feel like it is our responsibility to point out someone else's shadow, have been taking too much responsibility for things (AKA: trying to stay safe via control) since we were very, very tiny. I'm sorry you grew up that way and I'm sorry you've felt you had to do that. It's freaking exhausting. I'm trying to unlearn it too.

We can recognize the strong urge in ourselves to help, fix and mend and then we can just let it go. We can choose not to. Making this choice is a daily event, one that we will have to practice over and over again. We won't always be able to do it but when we can, we will have more energy, more joy and more peace in our lives. We will start to understand what it means to turn our focus back to ourselves and allow others to make their own decisions.

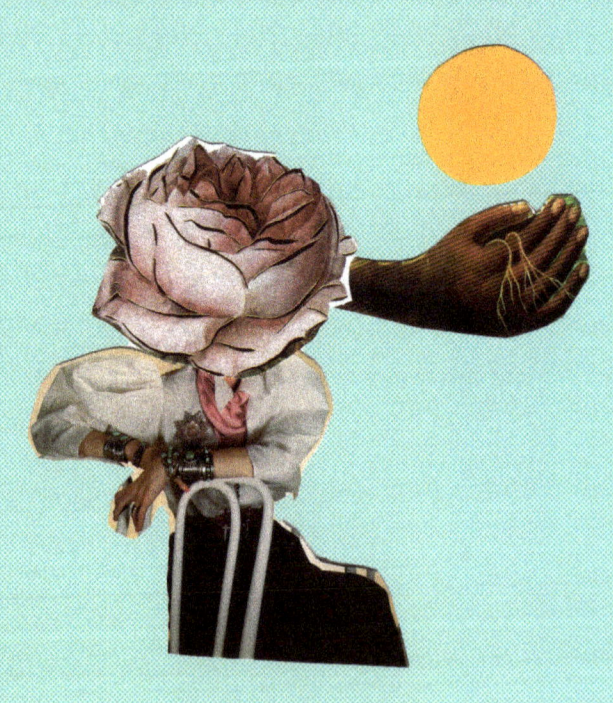

What If It Means Nothing / Shouldn't I Be Grateful?

We are so superstitious in our New Age circles. We want to make our pneumonia mean that we have not yet properly grieved our last relationship (because you know, the lungs according to Chinese Medicine symbolize grief) or that we are being punished for unfinished karmic business. We want to interpret the car accident we got into to mean we're on the wrong path and Spirit is trying to redirect us. We want to make our upside down tarot card mean that our day is going to be doomed or jinxed. We are terribly afraid that we are doing it *wrong*. We presume that experiencing joy and happiness means that Spirit approves of us and experiencing conflict and struggle means that Spirit is angry with us. I don't know about you but this sounds a lot like religion to me.

It actually sounds like religion mixed with the culture of sports in America. (I only know about sports fanaticism because my wife grew up in a family where watching the Yankees and rooting for the Yankees was non-negotiable. My wife told me that once, she made her mother stay in the bathroom during a Yankees game because they started winning when she went in. Only after the Yankees won the game was she allowed to come out of the bathroom and resume her daily life.)

We have become spiritually superstitious.

We want to make meaning of the misfortune in our lives. We want to read deeply into it and sometimes we can and need to. And other times, we create meaning of our experience that ultimately pressures us to be better, do better and figure out how to be better faster and right now.

I got pregnant when I was 23. I did not want to be pregnant. I was not ready to be a mother and had no resources (emotionally, spiritually or financially) to raise a child. As I was considering whether or not to have the baby, I called my brother from my parent's kitchen. As I sat in the kitchen, staring at the pink and purple flowered wallpaper, my brother said to me, "Just because the condom broke, doesn't mean you have to become a mother." I was freed when he said this to me. You mean the thin, poorly made condom was not a sign that I had to give my life over to the tiny seed living inside of me? I still had FREEDOM OF CHOICE?!

I immediately thought that my pregnancy was a sign. It *was* a sign, just not a sign for me to be a mother. It was a sign to wake me up to the fact that I had agency to choose the kind of life I wanted. The condom breaking did not mean that I was now destined to raise a baby, it meant that I was called to access my power and make a decision.

Also...

Please do not feel like you have to be grateful for the challenging things that happen to you. I do not have to access gratitude for my unwanted pregnancy when I actually feel grief and pain around it. I do not have to say something to myself like, *Well, you know, I am grateful for the pregnancy because it led me to realize that I have a passion for women's health.* We do not have to paint our challenging experiences with rose-colored brush strokes and we do not have to claim them as necessary karmic lessons. If and when we feel gratitude for them, great. But please, do not rush this process and think that in order to stay emotionally healthy, we have to only feel positive emotions.

As we know all too well, those of us in the Western world have a lot of GUILT. We feel guilty for our privilege, the lack of violence in our communities compared to other places in the world, our money, the time we spend experiencing pleasure and, of course, going to sound baths. We feel like we have so much that others do not have so why complain? WE SHOULD BE GRATEFUL — even for the bad things that happen.

Do you know how we suck all the pleasure and enjoyment out of life?

Continue to believe that if we force ourselves to be positive about the challenges in our lives, we somehow pay homage to people who are experiencing war, famine and violence in the world.

We are allowed to feel our shitty moments. We do not have to make meaning of them or find purpose in them. We do not have to find the silver lining and this doesn't mean that we are ungrateful for what we do have.

If the meaning you are making from a situation invokes a feeling of shame in you, explore a new meaning. And I mean, when you feel like a terrible person who can do no right, then you have not found the appropriate meaning for your situation. You have found a meaning rooted in guilt, shame and fear which will not move you one step closer to loving the reality of who you are.

When we find a meaning that allows our body to relax, take a deep breath, cry and even laugh, then we know we've hit gold. You're going to want to choose the meaning that is *harder* on yourself. It's just what we're used to as New Age enthusiasts. You are going to want to choose the meaning that feels like you are spiritually challenging yourself. But maybe, just choose the meaning that makes you feel like you can offer yourself deeper self-acceptance and a sense of relief. Maybe, that will feel like the biggest growth edge of all.

Bonus Section: How the New Age World Reminds Me of Barbieland

As I was finishing this little book, I couldn't leave you without saying just one more thing about the New Age world's relationship with negative emotions.

Anger is not allowed in the New Age world. Criticism is forbidden. Frustration is frowned upon. Disappointment is disastrous. These emotions seem to be the secret elixir that turn my New Age zealot friends into stone.

My rigorous New Age friends get defensive when I suggest an activity that they think could interfere with their positive vibes. I often get something like, "I don't even allow _____ (insert things like: reality television shows, sugar and any body lotion not containing CBD oil) into my house. I don't want that kind of energy/mindset/aura anywhere near me." I understand protecting yourself and protecting your space. I love saying NO and drawing boundaries (at least now I do). It's one of my favorite activities. But this is something different.

It goes along with the whole *what you think about or talk about becomes your reality* thing. Everywhere you step, the New Age world is stopping themselves from speaking, thinking and acting on seemingly negative thoughts and feelings.

I was chatting the other night to a new friend about my frustrations with the property I live on. (My wife and I have been remodeling our 5-acre homestead and farm in Northern New Mexico for the last year.) As I was explaining my frustrations to this friend, it became clear that my emotions were not going to sit well with them. They said to me, "But aren't you growing a lot? Aren't you learning so much? Don't you want to enjoy these moments that you're having?"

The ONLY THING that is appropriate to say to me in that situation is, "I hear you Jen. That sucks. Wow, you're doing a lot." That's literally all it takes. I do not need you to take my emotions away from me, wrap them in a tiny little ball and give them back to me with fairy dust sprinkled on top. I do not need to ask my Higher Self for a greater perspective nor do I need to integrate a deeper lesson in this moment.

Can we please stop doing this to one another?

My anger, my frustration—your anger, your frustration—is not a demon to be removed and banished. When we feel these challenging emotions, we become full-spectrum humans. It does not mean we are going to become resentful, bitter, hateful humans who can only feel anger. Anger is only *one* emotion on the wheel of emotions and I actually really love to feel it.

We seem to be hiding from "negative energy" as if we could somehow ward it off—if only we burned enough sage throughout our house THEN we would attract an abundance of love and light and have peaceful, joyful nighttime dreams full of small, tiny barnyard animals. I had two dreams this week where I was held at gunpoint and I am still full of gratitude for my life. A little violence in the dreamtime, does not take away my ability to appreciate life, feel positive and open my heart to love. It just means that my psyche rolls deep and hard and it always has.

Aspiring to only have positive emotions is like wishing to be a dragon instead of a human. It deprives us of the wonderful and horrible complexity of being human. Before Barbie (did you see the movie?) decides to become a real human, she closes her eyes and we see a montage of human life flash in front of her. She sees birth and life, marriage and love, sadness and fear and she still chooses it. She leaves Barbieland and becomes a real girl.

The New Age world is a lot like Barbieland to me. Everyone wakes up every morning and pretends to be in a good mood. They wave and smile and continue to fake being a vegan (I saw you eat that pork chop last week).

If *Barbie* taught us anything, it taught us that there is a breaking point in the happiness facade — fake happiness is not sustainable.

When we can handle pain and loss and anger, we will know that we can handle life. When we are no longer afraid that the hard emotions will destroy us and break us, we will know that we have built resiliency and Soul Grit. We don't need to wake up in Barbieland anymore.

We are stronger than that. We are more courageous than that and the only way we get through this life, is by being human.

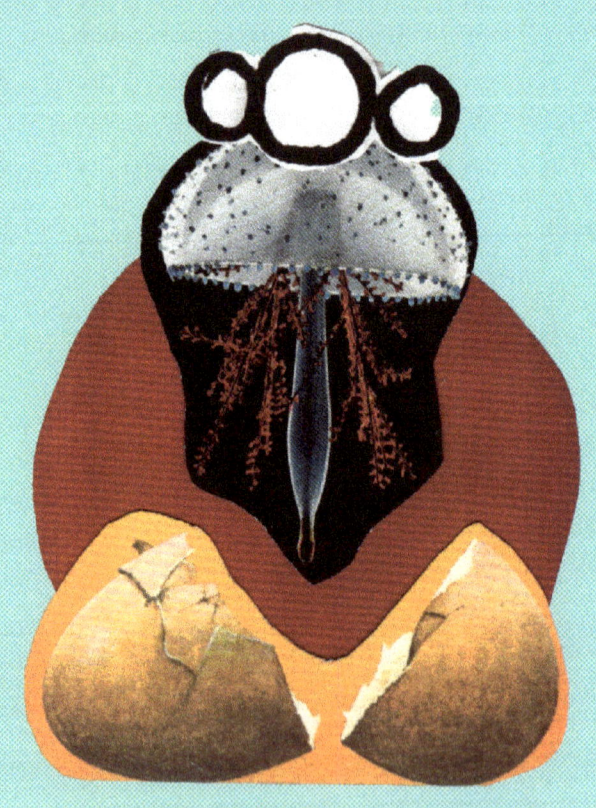

www.ingramcontent.com/pod-product-compliance
Lightning Source LLC
Chambersburg PA
CBHW040009080526
44586CB00028B/2942